Summer Job

PJ GRAY

LIFESKILLS IN ACTION
SOFT SKILLS

MONEY SKILLS

Living on a Budget | Road Trip
Opening a Bank Account | The Guitar
Managing Credit | High Cost
Using Coupons | Get the Deal
Planning to Save | Something Big

LIVING SKILLS

Smart Grocery Shopping | Shop Smart
Doing Household Chores | Keep It Clean
Finding a Place to Live | A Place of Our Own
Moving In | Pack Up
Cooking Your Own Meals | Dinner Is Served

JOB SKILLS

Preparing a Resume | Not Her Job
Finding a Job | Dream Jobs
Job Interview Basics | Job Ready
How to Act Right on the Job | Choices
Employee Rights | Not So Sweet

SOFT SKILLS

Emotional Intelligence | Bad Day
Communication | Tryout
Work Ethic | Summer Job
Problem-Solving | Bedtime Blues
Adaptability | Understudy

SADDLEBACK
EDUCATIONAL PUBLISHING
www.sdlback.com

ISBN: 978-1-68021-944-9
eBook: 978-1-64598-359-0

Printed in Malaysia

25 24 23 22 21   1 2 3 4 5

Another school year was over. Mona was ready for the beach. She couldn't wait to spend time with her friends.

Her mom had other ideas. She insisted that her daughter get a summer job. It would help with saving up for college.

"Mona!" her mom yelled. "Did you hear me? You are going to be late for work!"

"Okay, Mom!"

Mona held her phone to her ear. Her friend Emma was on the other end. As she talked, Mona checked her hair in the bedroom mirror. She was in no rush to leave.

"Sorry," Mona said. "Ugh. I hate this job. It's too much work."

"Why not quit?" Emma asked. "My beach party is soon. That way you won't miss it."

"I can't. I've only been working two weeks. Besides, the spending money is nice."

Mona's younger sister, Abby, entered the room.

"I have to go," Mona told Emma. "Catch you later." She hung up and turned to Abby. "What do you want? I'm late for work."

Abby had just gotten her driver's permit. Now she was looking for a job. Her goal was to save some money for a car.

"Did you speak to your boss?" Abby asked. "You said he might have a position open."

"Yes," Mona said. "I talked to him. He wants to meet you. Stop by the store tomorrow."

Mona worked at a small gift shop on the beach boardwalk. Her boss was Mr. Deen.

Abby was early for her interview the next day. Mr. Deen was impressed. Her thoughtful answers showed she wanted the job.

"The store will be very busy soon," he said. "I need a hard worker."

"You can count on me," Abby replied. "I am not afraid of hard work."

"Perfect," Mr. Deen said. "Can you start tomorrow? Mona will train you."

Abby nodded and thanked Mr. Deen for the job.

Later that night, she made a deal with her sister. Mona would drive her to work. In return, Abby would help pay for gas.

Abby's first week at work was busy. Mona trained her to stock the shelves. She also showed Abby how to use the cash register.

One day, Mr. Deen walked in during their shift. "Who cleaned the stockroom?" he asked.

Mona was afraid he was mad. She said nothing.

"That was me," Abby said. "I hope that was okay."

"Yes," Mr. Deen said. "Thank you. You did it without asking. I appreciate that."

Abby smiled. Mona rolled her eyes.

Mr. Deen had to go to the bank. He asked the girls to stock the shelves. "There are boxes of new T-shirts in the back. Price them, and then put them out."

Mona smiled. "Yes, sir. No problem."

Mr. Deen left.

Mona turned to Abby. "Get started on those boxes. I will stay at the cash register."

Abby worked hard on the new shipment. Not many customers came into the shop. She watched as Mona sat and texted her friends.

"You need to hurry," Mona said. "Mr. Deen wants that done today."

"Can you help me? These shirts need price tags."

"I can't," Mona replied. "My job is to watch the front of the store. Besides, I'm the boss for now. Mr. Deen said so. Get back to work."

Abby was mad but kept working. She watched Mona ring up a sale. The customer paid and left the store.

"Hey," Mona said to Abby. "I need to make a call. Can you work the register while I'm out?"

Mona walked into the back room. Abby went over to the register.

The customer came back into the store. He was holding money.

"May I help you?" Abby asked.

The man handed her a twenty-dollar bill. "The other girl gave me the wrong change."

"Pardon me?"

"She gave me an extra twenty in change. I just wanted to return it."

Abby was shocked. "Thank you so much. We appreciate your honesty."

The customer left. Mona returned to the front of the store.

Abby was upset. She showed Mona the money. "You gave that man an extra twenty dollars."

Mona laughed. "So what? It's no big deal."

"Yes, it is!"

Mona stopped smiling. "Are you going to tell Mr. Deen?"

Abby was silent.

"Just remember who got you this job."

Suddenly Mona's phone rang. It was one of her friends.

Abby turned to help another customer. He was looking for hats.

"Hey, Amy," Mona answered her phone. "Yeah, I'm at work. This place is the worst. I can't wait to get out of here."

Abby and the customer could hear Mona.

"Sorry about that," Abby said to the man. "Follow me. We have more hats over here. I think you will like them."

Mr. Deen returned later that day. Abby heard him speak to Mona.

"Great job with the shirts," he said.

"I worked as fast as I could," Mona replied.

Abby was upset that her sister took the credit. But she didn't say anything.

Mr. Deen asked to meet with the girls when the store closed.

"I'm going out of town next weekend," he said. "Mona will be in charge. Will the store be safe in your hands?"

"Yes, sir," both girls replied.

The next weekend came. Mona was up to her old tricks. She made Abby work extra hard. Meanwhile, Mona spent much of her time on the phone.

A woman entered the store. She wore a big pink hat. Abby turned to help her.

"I've got this," Mona told her sister. "Keep folding those beach towels."

The woman smiled. "Are these your only shirts?" she asked. "Do you have any more in the back?"

"No," Mona said. "There's no need to check the stockroom. We don't have your size. I can tell."

The woman stopped smiling. She stared at Mona.

Mona shrugged. "Sorry."

A moment later, Mona's phone buzzed. She read a text. Then she spoke to Abby.

"Hey," Mona said. "Watch the store. I'll be right back. I'm going to grab a drink with Emma."

"Wait," Abby said. "You already took a break. I can't be here alone. It's too busy."

"I will be right back. And don't tell anyone. Remember who got you this job."

Abby watched her sister leave the store. Then she turned to the woman and smiled.

"I am very sorry," Abby said. "Please let me help you."

The woman was grateful for Abby's help. She bought some gifts and left the store happy.

Mr. Deen returned on Monday morning. "I will be in my office," he said.

Just then the first customer entered the store. It was the woman Abby had helped on Saturday. She wore the same pink hat.

"Hello there!" the woman called out.

Abby froze. Did she return because of Mona?

Mr. Deen turned and smiled. "Donna! What are you doing here?"

"Surprise! I am here on vacation."

Mr. Deen laughed. "I didn't think you were coming this summer."

"I changed my mind," the woman said as they hugged. "Where were you this past weekend?"

"On a business trip," he said. Then he turned to Mona and Abby. "This is my older sister, Donna."

"We have met," Donna said. "I was here on Saturday."

Abby smiled. "It's nice to see you again."

Mona's face turned red. "Hello."

Donna nodded at them. She turned to Mr. Deen. "Let's grab a coffee."

"Great idea!" he replied.

"Go enjoy yourself," Abby said. "We will watch the store."

Mr. Deen smiled. "Thank you, Abby."

Later, Mr. Deen returned without Donna. He was frowning.

"May I speak with you?" he asked Mona.

Mona's face grew hot. She followed the owner into his office.

He sighed. "My sister told me a troubling story. You spoke rudely to her. Then you left the store suddenly. I would like to hear your side."

"Oh. Well, we didn't have shirts in her size. Then I went on break."

"What is the first rule here?"

"Treat every customer with respect."

"Yes. Your actions did not do that. I am disappointed. Mona, do you want this job?"

"I do."

"Then show me that. Please think about what happened. We will talk more later. For now, please watch the store. I would like to speak with Abby."

"Yes, sir," Mona said. She left looking shocked. When she saw her sister, she pointed to the office. "It's your turn. Don't be a tattletale."

Abby frowned. She went to see Mr. Deen.

"Hi, sir. Is there a problem?"

"Not with your work, Abby. Thank you for helping my sister. She told me how kind you were. I am very pleased with your attitude and work ethic. You are an asset to this store."

"Thank you," Abby said.

Mr. Deen continued. "Would you like to be the assistant store manager? It's more responsibility. But you'd also get a pay raise."

Abby smiled. "Wow! That would be an honor."

"Good. Let's go speak with your sister. She'll be reporting to you from now on."

Mona did not take the news well. She was quiet the rest of the day.

The drive home was particularly uncomfortable. Abby finally broke the silence.

"I'm sorry, Mona. You got me this job. I appreciate that. What can I do?"

Mona sighed. "This is on me, Abby. You have been working hard. I didn't take the job seriously. Mr. Deen did the right thing. Just give me some time to deal with it."

"Okay. And I promise not to be too hard on you," Abby joked.

"Thanks." Mona rolled her eyes. Then she smiled. "You're still my little sister. But I could learn a thing or two from you."

Employers appreciate employees with a strong work ethic. Want to learn more about how staying focused and working hard can really pay off?

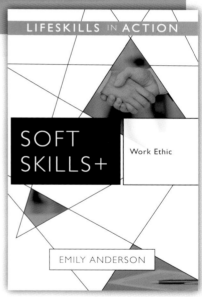

LIFESKILLS IN ACTION

SOFT SKILLS+

Work Ethic

EMILY ANDERSON

JUST *flip* THE BOOK!

LIFESKILLS IN ACTION

Work Ethic

EMILY ANDERSON

LIFESKILLS IN ACTION

SOFT SKILLS

SADDLEBACK
EDUCATIONAL PUBLISHING
www.sdlback.com

ISBN: 978-1-68021-944-9
eBook: 978-1-64598-359-0

Printed in Malaysia

25 24 23 22 21   1 2 3 4 5

D1551411

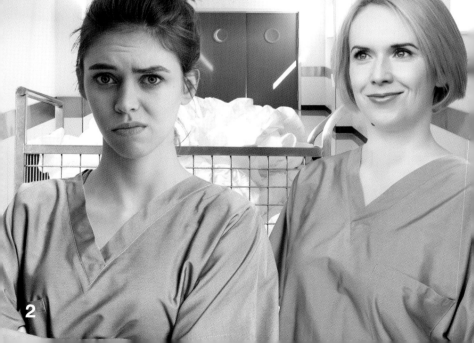

The hospital is busy.

There are many patients.

They all need fresh, clean bedding.

Some of the laundry workers feel **stressed.**

There's a lot of wash to do.

Sheets are heaped in carts.

Deb asks her coworker for help.

"Ami, can you give me a hand?

This cart is stuck."

"I hate that cart," Ami complains.

"It's always broken.

The front wheel is loose.

Someone should fix it."

"Help me," Deb says.

She shoves the cart.

It barely moves.

"Hold on," Ami says.

"I'm texting."

Deb rolls her eyes.

Ami came in late.

Now she's here **but isn't ready to work.**

"Fine," Deb says.

"I'll do it myself."

Moving the broken cart is hard.

Deb pushes and pulls.

She gets sweaty.

The cart moves slowly.

At last, it reaches the washer.

6

Deb loads the sheets.

She reaches for soap.

The jug is empty.

"Ami?" Deb calls.

"We're out of soap.

Would you get some, please?"

Ami grabs a jug.

It's leaking.

Not my problem, she thinks.

Soap drips.

The floor gets slick.

Ami **ignores it.**

They start the wash.

Then Deb turns to do the next task.

She slips and falls on the soapy floor.

"Ami, what happened?

Did you spill soap?"

"No," Ami lies.

"Really?"

"It wasn't my fault," Ami says.

"The jug had a hole in it."

Deb shakes her head.

"I could have been hurt.

Please clean it up."

Ami goes to get a mop.

When she comes back, she hears voices.

Deb is talking to their boss, Carla.

"What's the problem?" Carla asks.

"It's Ami," Deb says.

"She has a **poor work ethic.**"

"What do you mean?"

"Ami doesn't seem to care about the job.

Most days she is late.

Her work is sloppy.

She doesn't help out."

"That's not good," Carla says.

"I'll talk with her."

11

Ami drops the mop.

She's shocked.

They're talking about *her*!

Is she in trouble?

Deb spoke of a "work ethic."

Ami doesn't know the term.

The words seemed important.

What do they mean?

A work ethic is an inner guide.

It's a set of **values.**

Having one helps workers make good choices.

Most people care about their jobs.

Their actions show it.

They **strive to do well.**

Others notice their strong work ethic.

Look at Deb's choices.

What does she value?

Deb works hard.

She clearly cares about her job.

It's not so clear with Ami.

Does she value her job?

It doesn't seem like it.

Employers look for a strong work ethic.

Coworkers and customers appreciate it too.

Anyone can work hard.

You don't need special talents.

It just takes effort.

Here's one way to start.

Promise yourself to always be **on time.**

This shows you care about your job.

Buses can be late.

Sometimes cars break down.

Things come up.

Leave extra time just in case.

Think ahead.

Do you wear a uniform to work?

Wash it the night before.

Will you get hungry during your shift?

Eat before work.

Bring snacks too.

Do you need to find a ride home?

Finish texting before going in.

Be ready to work when your shift starts.

Tasks will come up.

They may not be on your list.

Be willing to help out.

Do more than you're asked.

This shows a strong work ethic.

There are some chores no one likes.

Offer to help anyway.

Someone has to do them.

Step up.

You can make a difference.

Think of work as a **team sport.**

Each person does their best.

Together, everyone succeeds.

Keep your team's goal in mind.

It can shape your outlook.

Look at Deb.

She wanted to do her job.

It was important to her.

Why?

Deb is part of a team.

The hospital needs clean sheets
and gowns.

They are part of patient care.

Deb is proud to help out.

She wants to do her best.

What about Ami?

She does not act like a team player.

Ami doesn't see the point in working.

That's why she's unhappy on the job.

Your **outlook** matters.

It shapes how you feel.

Others are affected too.

Avoid complaining.

That drags everyone down.

Smile.

This can boost your mood.

Others will smile back.

Always look on the bright side.

Problems will come up.

See them as chances for you to shine.

Think of Ami's story.

There was an issue at work.

The cart broke.

That slowed everything down.

What if Ami had tried to fix it?

She could have saved the day.

Here's some advice.

If something is broken, fix it.

Don't wait to be asked.

Take responsibility for things at work.

Stick with tasks until they are done.

Of course, even the best workers make mistakes.

That's okay.

Admit it when this happens.

Tell the truth.

Then try to **fix the problem.**

For example, Ami dripped soap.

But she didn't deal with it.

Instead she ignored it.

This created a risk.

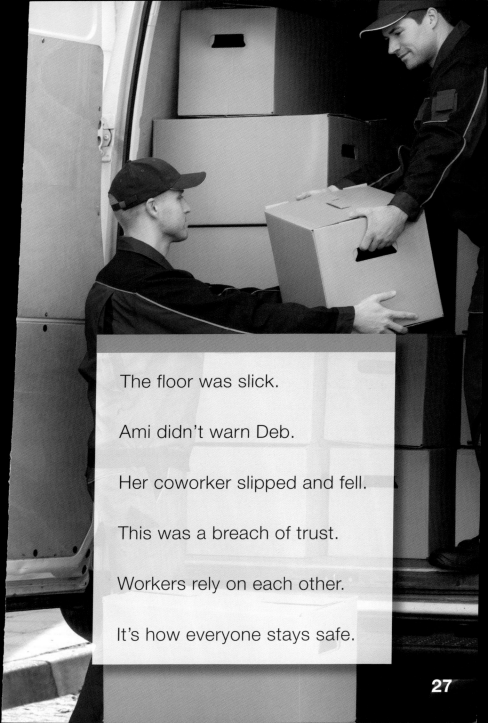

The floor was slick.

Ami didn't warn Deb.

Her coworker slipped and fell.

This was a breach of trust.

Workers rely on each other.

It's how everyone stays safe.

Be someone others can count on.

Good workers do the right thing.

Their words are true.

They act with **integrity.**

Even little things matter.

Don't sneak in extra breaks.

Employers consider this stealing.

They call it "time theft."

Stay focused during work hours.

Be trustworthy.

Take care of tools.

Don't waste supplies.

Protect resources.

Take care of people too.

Be kind.

Show respect.

Say "please" and "thank you."

Work can be fun when everyone gets along.

Some things are out of your control.

But you can choose how to respond.

Stay positive.

Offer to help.

The job may get tough.

Maybe a customer gets mad.

A machine could break.

New rules might trip you up.

Mona and Abby both get jobs at a gift shop for the summer. But the sisters have very different work ethics. Find out how that affects what happens in *Summer Job*. Want to read on?

JUST *flip* THE BOOK!

Don't worry.

Think about your values.

Let your work ethic guide you.

Make wise choices.

Then you will feel **proud** of your work no matter what.